DELIVER ME FROM EVIL A SPIRITUAL WARFARE & DELIVERANCE MANUAL

by
Robin Dinnanauth

ISBN: 978-1-365-16315-9

Contents

INTRODUCTION TO DELIVERANCE MESSAGE OF SALVATION

A Message of Salvation

Before you begin the process of deliverance from evil spirits, you first must be delivered from the power of sin. This can only be done by first having Jesus Christ as your personal Lord and Savior. You must be born again

Why must I be born again (saved)? The bible says in John 3:3 "Jesus answered and said to him, 'Most assuredly, I say to you, unless one is born again, he cannot see the kingdom of God.'" We all have sinned and fallen short of the glory of God (see Romans 3:23). The wages of sin is spiritual death, which is separation from God: Romans 6:23 says, "For the wages of sin is death, but the gift of God is eternal life in Christ Jesus our Lord. Being spiritually dead means that you are separated from God. If you die in this state, you will find yourself in eternal hell." The book of Revelations 20:15 says, "And anyone not found written in the Book of Life was cast into the lake of fire."

So what does it mean to be saved? When you are saved, you are as they say, born again! You are considered a new creation: 2 Corinthians 5:17 says, "Therefore, if anyone is in Christ, he is a new creation; old things have passed away; behold, all things have become new. You are adopted or born into the family of God ... a royal family!" The bible says in 1 John 3:1, "Behold what manner of love the Father has bestowed on us, that we should be called children of God! Therefore the world does not know us, because it did not know Him."

Your sins are removed from you and canceled from your account ... in other words, you are FORGIVEN! In the book of Micah 7:19 it is said, "He will again have compassion on us, And will subdue our iniquities. You will cast all our sins into the depths of the sea." Once your sins are forgiven, you are enclothed with the righteousness of God by faith in Christ Jesus. We see in Romans 3:22 it says, "Even the righteousness of God, through faith in Jesus Christ, to all and on all who believe. For there is no difference." You are seated with Christ in authority over all powers of the devil. And Ephesians 2:6 says, "And raised us up together, and made us sit together in the heavenly places in Christ Jesus." This means that you as a believer in Christ will be capable of casting out demons and healing sickness and disease (because you now have authority over sickness and disease, as well as all powers of the enemy). This authority is exercised through faith, so it is also important to cultivate and build your faith in order to fully take advantage of this benefit.

Mark 16:15–18 says, "And He said to them, 'Go into all the world and preach the gospel to every creature. He who believes and is baptized will be saved; but he who does not believe will be condemned. And these signs will follow those who believe: In My name they will cast out demons; they will speak with new tongues; they will take up serpents; and if they drink anything deadly, it will by no means hurt them; they will lay hands on the sick, and they will recover.'"

Yes, that means that you as a believer in Christ can go fourth and cast out demons and heal the sick. Why? Because you have been given authority over sickness, disease, and over all powers of the devil! Now don't get me wrong: the more you understand about the ministry of deliverance and healing, the more effective you will be at ministering to others in those areas, but as for the authority needed to cast out demons and heal the sick ... that belongs to you naturally as a child of God.

Now the *question* is what should you do to be saved? Although we cannot pay for our sins, Jesus' shed blood is more than enough! Jesus truly did stand in the gap for us when He went to the cross. In the Old Testament (before Jesus came), they would sacrifice animals to cover their sins, but now that Jesus paid the price, we no longer need to perform sacrifices. In the

Old Testament, we could only cover our sins with the blood of animals, but the blood of Jesus actually removes our sin … it erases it from our account all together! Hebrews 10:4 says "For it is not possible that the blood of bulls and goats could take away sins." The blood of Christ actually takes sin away, so much so, that God Himself chose not to remember our failures! Hebrews 10:17 says "Their sins and their lawless deeds I will remember no more."

The blood of Christ was shed for our sins, and through faith in the work which was done for us, we can be freely justified … that is, made right with God: Romans 3:24–26 says, "Being justified freely by His grace through the redemption that is in Christ Jesus, whom God set forth as a propitiation by his blood, through faith, to demonstrate His righteousness, because in His forbearance God had passed over the sins that were previously committed, to demonstrate at the present time His righteousness, that He might be just and the justifier of the one who has faith in Jesus." Notice that the word "justified" in the above verse takes us back to the Greek word dikaioo, which means, "to render (that is, show or regard as) just or innocent." That means that you are made innocent … as if you've never sinned! That's how clean that you can be through faith in the work that Jesus did for us on the cross.

Your first step is to believe in your heart that Jesus Christ is the Son of God, that he came to earth (living in a human body), was crucified and died for your sins, and then rose again on the third day. John 3:16–17 says, "For God so loved the world that He gave His only begotten Son, that whoever believes in Him should not perish but have everlasting life. For God did not send His Son into the world to condemn the world, but that the world through Him might be saved."

Acts 16:30–31 says, "And he brought them out and said, 'Sirs, what must I do to be saved?' So they said, 'Believe on the Lord Jesus Christ, and you will be saved, you and your household.'"

Second, confess with your mouth the Lord Jesus Christ (affirm your belief verbally). This is usually what we refer to as the sinner's prayer. Romans 10:9 says, "That if you confess with your mouth the Lord Jesus and believe in your heart that God has raised Him from the dead, you will be saved." An example of the sinner's prayer would be, "Lord Jesus, I believe that you are the son of God and that you came to earth and died for my sins and rose again on the third day. I confess I am a sinner and in need of your salvation. I come to you now and ask that you will come into my life, be my Lord and savior, and forgive me of my sins. In Jesus' name, amen!"

The Bible also speaks of water baptism, and I believe all believers should be baptized. This is symbolic of being washed from the darkness of your past, putting away the old you and being raised to new life in Christ Jesus: Romans 6:4 says "Therefore we were buried with Him through baptism into death, that just as Christ was raised from the dead by the glory of the Father, even so we also should walk in newness of life."

Understand that you are not saved by works but by faith in Jesus Christ. It is important to know we are not saved by our works, but by faith in Christ Jesus and the work that He did for us: Titus 3:5 says, "Not by works of righteousness which we have done, but according to His mercy He saved us, through the washing of regeneration and renewing of the Holy Spirit." Our sins are paid for by the Blood of Jesus and nothing less will do: Matthew 26:28 says, "For this is My blood of the new covenant, which is shed for many for the remission of sins." Do not try to 'earn' your salvation or forgiveness of sins ... you must realize that it is by faith in Christ that saves you, not your works! Good works should follow naturally as you grow in your relationship with God (after all, we will become more like Him as we grow spiritually), but that by no means will justify you of past sins. The question is asked: does God really forgive sins freely? Yes! There are a couple accounts in the Bible I would like to point out: Luke 7:47–50 says

"Therefore I say to you, her sins, which are many, are forgiven, for she loved much. But to whom little is given, the same loves little." Then He said to her, 'Your sins are forgiven.' And those who sat at the table with Him began to say to themselves, 'Who is this who even forgives sins?' Then He said to the woman, 'Your faith has saved you. Go in Peace.'"

Another great story is when Jesus was on the cross and the man next to him (a murderer) basically asked Jesus to remember him when He enters his kingdom: Luke 23:42–43says "Then he said to Jesus, 'Lord, remember me when You come into Your kingdom.' And Jesus said to him, 'Assuredly, I say to you, today you will be with Me in Paradise.'" Did either of those people work to earn their forgiveness? No!

Jesus Loves you even before you accept Him! Even before we accept Jesus, He loves us ... but that doesn't mean we are saved, until we accept His son and believe in the work that He did for us on the cross! Romans 5:8 says, "But God demonstrates His own love toward us, in that while we were still sinners, Christ died for us."

Will God forgive or accept me? Yes, providing you will come unto Him! Jesus told us clearly He will by no means turn down anybody who turns to Him in repentance: John 6:37 says, "All that the Father gives Me will come to Me, and the one who comes to Me I will by no means cast out." God tells us clearly that if we confess our sins, He is faithful and just and will forgive us of ALL unrighteousness—meaning anything you've done wrong that you can take before the Lord, you can receive forgiveness for! 1 John 1:9 adds, "If we confess our sins, He is faithful and just to forgive us our sins, and to *cleanse us from all unrighteousness*."

You are a threefold being. You are a threefold person. You are a spirit who lives in a physical body and possesses a soul (mind, will, and emotions). The moment you accept Jesus, your spirit is reborn and made new. 2 Corinthians 5:17 says, "Therefore, if anyone is in Christ, he is a new creation; old things have passed away; behold, all things have become new." But what are not made new are your soul (mind, will, and emotions) and your body (physical). These two things can carry corruption over from your past life, and should be renewed and transformed as you grow and cultivate your new relationship with God. The Bible tells us to be transformed by the renewing of our minds, which is by the washing of the Word of God. Spending time in God's Word on a daily basis is like washing yourself spiritually. It will change the way you think, build your faith, and help you grow. Romans 12:2 says, "And do not be conformed to this world, but be transformed by the renewing of your mind, that you may prove what is that good and acceptable and perfect will of God."

Ephesians 5:25–27, "Husbands, love your wives, just as Christ also loved the church and gave Himself for her, that He might sanctify and cleanse her with the washing of water by the word, that He might present her to Himself a glorious church, not having spot or wrinkle or any such thing, but that she should be holy and without blemish."

There are also times when you may require deliverance ministry to get rid of any unclean spirits that have attached themselves to your soul or body. If you are being tormented, depressed, fearful, or have bondages of any kind, then I encourage you to seek deliverance from those things. One of the common reasons why so many Christians today are defeated and powerless in the kingdom is because they neglect the transforming of their soul and body through the renewing of their mind, the tearing down of strongholds and seeking proper deliverance ministry.

Not only were our bondages (infirmities) paid for by the work of Christ, but also our physical healing.

What do I do now that I am saved? After being born again, it is important to cultivate your new relationship with Christ Jesus. You do this by spending time in God's Word on a daily basis. I recommend starting out in the book of John in the New Testament. As you meditate (that is, to dwell upon) on God's Word, it will begin to change the way you think. Your mind will be renewed and transformed and strongholds (old thinking patterns) begin to come down. This is vital to your spiritual freedom and wholeness! Romans 12:2 says, "And do not be conformed to this world, but be transformed by the renewing of your mind, that you may prove what is that good and acceptable and perfect will of God."

Ephesians 5:25–27 states, "Husbands, love your wives, just as Christ also loved the church and gave Himself for her, *that He might sanctify and cleanse her with the washing of water by the word*, that He might present her to Himself a glorious church, not having spot or wrinkle or any such thing, but that she should be holy and without blemish.

Ephesians 3:17–19 says, "That Christ may dwell in your hearts through faith; that you, being rooted and grounded in love, May be able to comprehend with all saints what is the width and length and depth and height—*to know the love of Christ which passes knowledge; that you may be filled with all the fullness of God.*"

Finally, seek to receive your deliverance and baptism of the Holy Spirit. This is beyond the gift of salvation and an extremely powerful gift that God wants to give you now that you have become a believer in Christ.

WHAT IS DELIVERANCE?

Deliverance is being set free from spiritual bondages and barriers that hold us back from walking in the victory that Jesus won on the cross for us at Calvary. Put more bluntly, it is the driving out of evil spirits by the authority of the Lord Jesus Christ.

It is an essential process probably all Christians need to ensure they can be totally set free. It is wrong to assume that once you give your life to Jesus Christ and receive the Holy Spirit, you are automatically delivered from those demonic strongholds that hold you down. One of the many benefits of being a Christian is that only Christians filled with the Holy Spirit can be delivered! If you are not a Holy Spirit-filled Christian and a deliverance is performed, then you do not have the protection and guidance from the Holy Spirit to stop any demonic influence from returning and interfering in your life which could make things worse.

"When an unclean spirit goes out of a man, he goes through dry places, seeking rest, and finds none. Then he says. 'I will return to my house from which I came.' And when he comes, he finds it empty, swept, and put in order. Then he goes and takes with him seven other spirits more wicked than himself, and they enter and dwell there; and the last state of that man is worse than the first. So shall it also be with this wicked generation." Matthew 12:43–45

Despite what many people think, deliverance is not about the demons. It is about being set free in Jesus' name. When deliverance is ministered properly, **Jesus is glorified** and our lives are changed for the better.

HOW DEMONS GAIN ACCESS IN A PERSON'S LIFE

Demons can gain access to a person's life through doors, vows, and other spiritual signatures that give them legal rights to invade their life. Even believers can have demons, because demons most often invade the soul, while the spirit of the person is God's property.

So the question is how demons gain access in your life. This, I believe, is the most important part of deliverance. It is important to find out what opened the door to the enemy so that you can close it and void their legal rights from bothering you. There are a number of ways demons can gain access: through sins, ancestral sins (which causes ancestral curses), unforgiving heart (which blocks God's forgiveness toward us), dabbling in the occult, demonic vows, fear, etc.

Sins, especially willful sins! When we commit sin, it gives the enemy a legal right to affect or bother us one way or another. The deeper the sin, the bigger the door opened to the devil. When a person allows unholy thoughts to enter their mind, it can open the door to a demon of lust, which eventually causes the person to commit adultery, and the matter is compounded. It starts when the enemy tempts us to think the wrong thing, then when we accept it and make it a habit, it opens the door for the enemy to move in further, then behind the bad habit which can be formed lies a demonic compulsion that isn't easily resisted. If the person continues down this path, he continues to open more doors to the enemy, and eventually that person finds himself committing adultery, rape, etc., because the feelings and desires the demons push on that person are irresistible. Once he commits those sins, mega doors are then opened, and the problem is like a snowball going down the hill. Sin opens the door to demons, which push us in the direction to more sins, which open us wider to more demons, etc.

Soul ties! It is possible for two persons to share spiritual ties (open doors). For example, committing fornication or adultery can create an unhealthy soul tie and result in demonic bondage. If that person had demons tormenting them and you had sex with them, it unites the two persons, and therefore a soul tie is created, and the demons tormenting that person can also have rights to torment you. I do not believe this applies to married couples, because there is no unhealthy soul tie created from sex within marriage.

Demonic vows - A demonic vow can be like a spiritual signature that the enemy uses as a legal right to gain access into our lives. Demonic vows can be made consciously or unconsciously. Often when a person joins a cult coven (a group of witches), they are required to make vows with the devil. Demonic vows can be made unconsciously just by dabbling with the occult. Just by getting curious about the occult and reading forbidden materials (including horoscopes) can give the enemy your spiritual signature; it tells the enemy that you're interested.

Unforgiveness - When we don't forgive others, God won't forgive us. When God doesn't forgive us, our sins are left as they they were, which can give the enemy legal rights into our lives. Read Matthew 18:23–35: "Therefore the kingdom of heaven is like a certain king who wanted to settle accounts with his servants. And when he had begun to settle accounts, one was brought to him who owed him ten thousand talents. But as he was not able to pay, his master commanded that he be sold, with his wife and children and all that he had, and that payment be made. The servant therefore fell down before him, saying, 'Master, have patience with me, and I will pay you all.' Then the master of that servant was moved with compassion, released him, and forgave him the debt. "But that servant went out and found one of his fellow servants who owed him a hundred denarii; and he laid hands on him and took him by the throat, saying, 'Pay me what you owe!' So his fellow servant fell down at his feet and begged him, saying, 'Have patience with me, and I will pay you all.' And he would not, but went and threw him into prison till he should pay the debt. So when his fellow servants saw what had been done, they were very grieved, and came and told their master all that had been done. Then his master, after he had called him, said to him, 'You wicked servant! I forgave you all that debt because you begged me. Should you not also have had compassion on your fellow servant, just as I had pity on you?' And his master was angry, and delivered him to the torturers until he should pay all that was due to him. So My heavenly Father also will do to you if each of you, from his heart, does not forgive his brother his trespasses."

And keep in mind that the tormentors they are referring to are demons. The legal ground the enemy may be standing on to torment you may very well be rooted in unforgiveness! I've heard that the single most common reason people aren't healed is because they are holding unforgiveness in their hearts, and I believe it! Forgiveness is not an option—it's a necessity!

Ancestral sins - When you involve yourself in the deeper sins or the occult world, you not only open demonic doors in your own life, but also in the lives of your children and grandchildren (Exodus 20:5: "You shall not bow down to them nor serve them. For I, the LORD your God, am a jealous God, visiting the iniquity of the fathers upon the children to the third and fourth generations of those who hate Me."). If your ancestors have committed gross sins or been involved in the occult, then you need to confess those sins (to the best of your ability ... God knows your heart) to God and ask Him for forgiveness (Leviticus 26:40–42: "But if they confess their iniquity and the iniquity of their fathers, with their unfaithfulness in which they were unfaithful to Me, and that they also have walked contrary to Me, and that I also have walked contrary to them and have brought them into the land of their enemies; if their uncircumcised hearts are humbled, and they accept their guilt—then I will remember My covenant with Jacob, and My covenant with Isaac and My covenant with Abraham I will remember; I will remember the land."). Even though you personally aren't guilty of those sins, they may have caused curses in your life, and those curses need to be broken.

Childhood rejection - Much demonic bondage is caused during childhood. For example, if a parent shows rejection toward their child, a spirit of rejection may enter. The child must forgive his/her parent, and the spirit of rejection needs to be cast out.

Points of weakness - When the person experiences any weakness, such as emotional shock, physical trauma or fearful experiences during childhood and other areas by which the natural walls of defense in the physical, spiritual, or emotional system of a person are weakened.

Spoken self-curses - The words we say have spiritual value. The Bible says to bless and not curse, and that the tongue has the power of life and death. If you walk around saying, "I wish I could just die," a demon may hear you and can go to God and say, "Look, she wants to die!" and here comes a spirit of death.

SHUTTING THE ENTRANCES FROM DEMONIC SPIRITS

If you try to cast a demon out without first closing the doors that he used to gain access, then he probably won't leave, and your chances of encountering a manifestation increase. It is wise to first remove the rights that the enemy has, then cast him out!

Repent - If you haven't already received Jesus as your Savior, you must do so before you are entitled to the freedom that Jesus died to give you. We need to take our sins to the Lord and obtain forgiveness. If we confess our sins, He is faithful and just to forgive us our sins, as 1 John 1:9 says: "If we confess our sins, He is faithful and just to forgive us our sins and to cleanse us from all unrighteousness."

If we are breaking a generational curse, I believe it is a good idea to confess your ancestors' sins to the best of your ability to the Lord and ask Him for forgiveness. Even though we aren't personally guilty for our ancestor's sins, the Bible talks about confessing them to the Lord. Leviticus 26:40–42 explains thus: "But if they confess their iniquity of their fathers, with their unfaithfulness in which they were to Me, and that they also have walked contrary to Me, and that I also have walked contrary to them and have brought them into the land of their enemies; if their uncircumcised hearts are humbled, and they accept their guilt—then I will remember My covenant with Jacob, and My covenant with Isaac and My covenant with Abraham I will remember; I will remember the land." I do not believe you need to confess every tiny thing they did, but rather the bigger sins that could have opened doors for curses in the family tree. Things such as adultery, fornication, occult dabbling, and things of that nature are good examples of the deeper sins that cause curses. If the Holy Spirit leads you to confess something, then do it!

Forgive others! It is 100 percent vital that we forgive those who have wronged us. This allows God to forgive us (Matthew 6:14: "For if you forgive men their trespasses, your heavenly Father will also forgive you."). Holding unforgiveness in our hearts blocks us from receiving God's forgiveness toward us (Matthew 6:15: "But if you do not forgive men their trespasses, neither will your Father forgive your trespasses."). Unforgiveness is a major cause of demonic bondage, and one of the common reasons a demon may refuse to leave and have legal rights to stay. When you think of somebody, how do you view him or her? Do you see their wrongs and immediately remember the ways they hurt you? Or do you look upon them with love and compassion, and see them as another person whom Christ died for? Remember, Jesus commanded us to love one another as He has loved us (John 15:12: "This is My commandment, that you love one another as I have loved you.") And if we don't love one another, then we abide in death (1 John 3:14: "We know that we have passed from death to life, because we love the brethren. He who does not love his brother abides in death."). In 1 John 3:15 it says, "Whoever hates his brother is a murderer, and you know that no murderer has eternal life abiding in him." If you hold unforgiveness and hate within your heart against one another, then your sins aren't forgiven (Matthew 6:15: "But if you do not forgive men their trespasses, neither will your Father forgive your trespasses.") and you don't have eternal life! He who doesn't love one another doesn't even know God (1 John 4:8: "He who does not love does not know God, for God is love. You can't love God and hate thy brother"; 1 John 4:20 adds: "If someone says, 'I love God,' and hates his brother, he is a liar; for he who does not love his brother whom he has seen, how can[a] he love God whom he has not seen?")

Renounce - Closing the door is often done through renouncing whatever opened the door and maybe the demon(s) that have entered through the door being opened. For example, if there was a door opened through dabbling with horoscopes, then you could renounce your interest reading those horoscopes, and if the 'spirit of poverty' came upon you because of what you did, then you might renounce the spirit of poverty. Unhealthy soul ties also need to be renounced.

Destroy physical objects - Often there are items that can give the enemy legal rights to torment us. These items are things such as rings, gifts between two persons who were involved in a sin together (adultery, fornication, etc.), idols, false gods or anything related to the occult. Those items causing spiritual bondage must be destroyed! If the item is valuable and is not evil in itself, say a ring that was given as a love gift from one person to another while committing adultery, then the item may be sold. This breaks the legal grounds that the enemy is using through those items to torment us.

Tear down strongholds - Strongholds are incorrect thinking patterns that demons use to their advantage.

Expel - This is done when we take authority over the enemy and break the curses and/or demonic vows we've made with him. Any vows or dabbling with the enemy needs to be renounced and the power of those vows needs to be broken in Jesus' name. When all the doors have been closed on the enemy, it's time to command the evil spirits to leave in the name of Jesus.

Break. After we repent, we have the right to cancel or renounce any legal hold the enemy had over us. The **yoke of bondage** can be broken off our lives. God loves to see us come to the place where yokes are broken—and it thoroughly frustrates the enemy! It is quite common to use **anointing oil** when praying for someone's deliverance. There is nothing supernatural about the oil. It is, however, representative of someone who is very **supernatural**. That one is Jesus, the Messiah, and the anointed one as Isaiah 61:1 says: "The Spirit of the Lord GOD is upon Me, Because the LORD has anointed Me To preach good tidings to the poor; He has sent Me to heal the brokenhearted, To proclaim liberty to the captives, And the opening of the prison to those who are bound." The oil serves as a point of reference to build faith. We are declaring that repentance has taken place, the enemy has been renounced, and now, with the authority of Jesus' name and because of the power of His death and resurrection, the yoke of bondage is broken. "The yoke will be destroyed because of the anointing oil" (Isaiah 10:27: "It shall come to pass in that day, That his burden will be taken away from your shoulder, And his yoke from your neck, And the yoke will be destroyed because of the anointing oil.") At this point of breaking, a struggle begins and ends. It is the primary place of confrontation with the enemy, and now the light of Jesus is shining where darkness once ruled. The enemy has been found out and cast out. It is a great time of freedom and joy. I have seen multiplied thousands of people set free by this simple application of God's Word.

OUR GOD-GIVEN AUTHORITY THROUGH JESUS CHRIST

However, it is crucially important for believers going into battle to be aware of their authority in Christ. Deliverance is not a benign activity. We are dealing with **disobedient spirits**. These demons will use any opportunity to bluff, intimidate, lie or oppose. I have very little faith in my own ability. But I know Jesus, and I am convinced that when He said He was giving us authority, He was telling the truth. (Mark 16:17: "And these signs will follow those who believe: In My name they will cast out demons; they will speak with new tongues.") Jesus commended the centurion who believed that if Jesus gave the word, his servant would be healed. This centurion understood authority and knew the power of the one giving the healing command. We must also understand and believe in this authority. It is not a haughty authority but a humble, honest response to who Jesus is and what He has done. In the natural realm, the reason we stop our car when the lights on a police car are flashing behind us is not because of who's inside but because of what he represents. The officer in that car may be on the job for the first day. He might be slight of build. He might not be feeling well, yet, if he flashes his lights, we stop. Why? He represents the law. He is coming in the name of the law. If we resist, we are resisting to our own calamity. The entire judicial system will back up the police officer. In the spiritual realm, our authority is derived not from our own strength but from the One who granted it to us. Our authority is no less because we're new at it or because we're young or frail or not very wise. Spiritual authority depends not upon us but upon Him.

Deliverance prayer is so different from what people are used to. Normally when praying for someone else we close our eyes, bow our heads, and speak words of encouragement and blessing. When praying deliverance our eyes are wide open, our words are not directed to God; we are launching a frontal attack against the enemy. We are coming against whatever demon has deceived and manipulated you. This is a brand-new experience for many. Demons have ravaged God's people. Like mad dogs, they have sought to steal, kill, and destroy.

A **righteous anger** is appropriate when coming against such evil forces. Boldness to confront and put to flight is quite in order. I'm not speaking about volume but rather a focused and assertive intensity—looking the enemy in the face and making it clear that you know your authority in Christ and will accept no compromise. The demon must leave! You have the authority to roust the enemy from your own life as well as the lives of others.

PREPARATIONS AND PRECAUTIONS FOR YOUR DELIVERANCE PROCESS

This is a basic step-by-step outline of how to go about self-deliverance. This is not a complete set of instructions that will work for everybody, so if you need to be freed from heavier bondages, you may be better off consulting with an actual deliverance minister if you are able to locate one. These instructions will give you a good idea how to drive demons out of yourself. It is recommended that you read up further on this subject before attempting to run yourself through deliverance.

The limits of self-deliverance: Self deliverance is very helpful in many situations where a deliverance minister isn't available to minister to you, and you can be set free from many bondages simply by running yourself through a self-deliverance. However, it can be limited if compared to a regular deliverance session.

Precaution: If you have come out of heavy or active involvement in occult or Satanism, you would be better off seeing somebody else to minister deliverance to you (an experienced deliverance minister), because the demons encountered in those situations are usually much stronger and are best off handled by somebody else. If you begin to feel like you are losing control as a demon manifests, then stop and seek help from an experienced deliverance minister.

Predeliverance prayer: As with any deliverance, it is good to pray that the Holy Spirit would show you what the roots to the problem are and what needs to be done. Pray for His continual guidance and strength during the deliverance session. It is often helpful to ask God to send angels to assist in the deliverance. They can play a powerful role in helping you flush the demons out.

Warning to nonbelievers: Deliverance is for believers (Matthew 15:22–28: "And behold, a woman of Canaan came from that region and cried out to Him, saying, 'Have mercy on me, O Lord, Son of David! My daughter is severely demon-possessed.' But He answered her not a word. And His disciples came and urged Him, saying, 'Send her away, for she cries out after us.' But He answered and said, 'I was not sent except to the lost sheep of the house of Israel.' Then she came and worshiped Him, saying, 'Lord, help me!' But He answered and said, 'It is not good to take the children's bread and throw it to the little dogs.' And she said, 'Yes, Lord, yet even the little dogs eat the crumbs which fall from their masters' table.' Then Jesus answered and said to her, 'O woman, great is your faith! Let it be to you as you desire.' And her daughter was healed from that very hour.") and is not fit for unbelievers (those who are outside the covenant). If you aren't a Christian, I wouldn't even attempt a deliverance, because it's like stirring up a hornet's nest. First accept Jesus, then seek deliverance. This way, you can prevent the demons from returning with several more and even worse evil spirits as Jesus warns in Matthew 12:43–45, "When an unclean spirit goes out of a man, he goes through dry places, seeking rest, and finds none. Then he says, 'I will return to my house from which I came.' And when he comes, he finds it empty, swept, and put in order. Then he goes and takes with him seven other spirits more wicked than himself, and they enter and dwell there; and the last state of that man is worse than the first. So shall it also be with this wicked generation." If you aren't a believer, I wouldn't even try to cast a demon out of anybody, as we can see in Acts 19:13–16: "Then some of the itinerant Jewish exorcists took it upon themselves to call the name of the Lord Jesus over those who had evil spirits, saying 'We exorcise you by the name of Jesus whom Paul preaches.' [14] Also there were seven sons of Sceva, a Jewish chief priest, who did so. And the evil spirit answered and said, 'Jesus I know, and Paul I know; but who are you?' Then the man in whom the evil spirit was leaped on them, overpowered them, and prevailed against them, so that they fled out of that house naked and wounded." It's not wise to cast demons out if you aren't a child of God! They did not have authority in Jesus because they were unbelievers and seven men got thrown out of the house naked and beaten by the demon. As you can see, it's not wise or safe to attempt deliverance without Jesus in your life!

Prayer and fasting: Prayer and fasting always helps in preparing you for deliverance. Jesus said that some kinds of demons will only come forth through prayer and fasting. Prayer and fasting builds your faith to the higher levels required to cast some demons out.

KNOW YOUR RIGHTS - If you don't believe what is rightfully yours, it's going to be hard to claim it. Some of the things you need to have down pat are knowing your sins are forgiven, knowing you are a child of God, and knowing you have authority over the demons.

You need to understand who you are in Christ. This sounds simple and is often overlooked, but is VITAL to your deliverance. If you don't really believe you are who you are, then you won't have the faith to stand on who you are and claim what is rightfully yours. If you don't really know that you're a child of a king, you won't feel like a prince, and you won't act like a prince. And how are you supposed to defeat the enemy when you don't think like a child of God should think? If you struggle with this, you need to tear down one or more strongholds.

You need to know that your sins are forgiven. If you have guilt hanging over your head, then it will greatly hinder your ability to stand up to the enemy with a clear conscience and stand up for what is rightfully yours. Guilt is a door opener and keeper, and the enemy often uses it as a base to launch all sorts of attacks against God's children. You need to understand the nature of God and how freely Jesus wants to forgive you of ALL your sins. Luke 7:47 that says, "Therefore I say to you, her sins, which are many, are forgiven, for she loved much. But to whom little is forgiven, the same loves little," is one of my favorite verses the Lord showed me one time when I needed to learn this principle. It tells of how freely Jesus forgave a very sinful woman from all her sins without hesitation! Another good story on the forgiveness of our sins when we turn to God in repentance is found in Luke 15. If you struggle with obsessive guilt even after repenting of your sins and turning from them, then you need to tear down one or more strongholds.

You need to have a correct perception of God and your relationship with Him. If you see God incorrectly, you're going to be an easy target for the enemy. If you see God as a cruel taskmaster, you'll act like He's a cruel taskmaster and you will put up walls that will block you from feeling God's love. Furthermore, the enemy moves in with the power of suggestion (little things he whispers into your thought-life), and terrorizes the daylights out of you. If you think of anybody (husband, wife, boss, etc.) as a cruel mean taskmaster, it puts up a wall and you see that person differently, don't you? Even though you could be completely wrong in your perception of them, to you they are a taskmaster, and therefore you shut them out of your heart. This is what we do to God when we see Him as a cruel and distant taskmaster. We cut ourselves off from experiencing and feeling His love. If you don't feel God loves you, then you need to back up and take a moment to review how you are perceiving Him. Many people struggle with this, and it is a stronghold that needs to be torn down.

You need to know the authority you have been given by God over the enemy. You as a believer have been given authority over all powers of the enemy, and have been given the authority to bind and loose in the spiritual realm. You exercise your authority through a spoken word in faith; just as Jesus cast demons out with His word, you can also cast demons out with your word, which is backed by the authority that Jesus gave us as believers. You have the authority whether your feel like it not as long as you are a believer. It is important to know that your authority is accessed through faith, and therefore the more you believe in your authority, the more of it you will be able to exercise. Mark 16:17 tells us that those who believe will be casting out demons in His name!

As I mentioned above several times, there's often the need to tear down strongholds in our lives. There's an excellent teaching just on *strongholds* that you may want to go through before attempting a self-deliverance if you sense that there's any strongholds that need to be torn down.

BREAK LEGAL GROUNDS - I believe this is one of the most important parts of the deliverance process. It is important to find out what opened the door to the enemy, so we can close it and void their legal right to bother us. There are a number of ways he can gain access—through sins, ancestral sins (which causes ancestral curses), unforgiving heart (which blocks God's forgiveness toward us), dabbling in the occult, demonic vows, fear, etc.

IDENTIFY THE AREAS OF BONDAGE IN YOUR LIFE - It's important to know what areas of your life are in bondage, and have a good idea of exactly what you are seeking to be set free from. Make a list of the things you want to be freed from. Know exactly what you want to be set free from, then try to identify the 'open door' that allowed the enemy to move into that area of your life. When did it start? If you had it your entire life and your parents or grandparents struggled with the same or similar problem, then it was likely generational. Often you can locate what opened up the bondage if you look back around the time in your life when it started. It's always a good idea to become familiar with the various ways the enemy can gain access into our lives. A good understanding of Legal Rights and Strongholds is always helpful. There is a Deliverance Questionnaire in this book to help you identify areas of bondage in your life. This can be helpful to even an inexperienced person who has a general understanding of legal rights and strongholds.

It's always a good idea to make some lists pertaining to your bondage. A list of legal rights is good, and can help you keep track as you are going through the list and breaking up those legal grounds. A list of the areas of bondage in your life is always a good idea. A list of strongholds is also a good idea to keep track of. If you need further deliverance from another minister or need more deliverance in the future (not all bondages are broken in one session—it often takes multiple sessions to completely set a person free), it can be very helpful to keep track of what is going on. If you seek further ministering from an experienced minister, presenting those lists to him or her can give them a good quick look into your situation and can save them time trying to uncover the areas of bondage in your life.

CASTING THE DEMONS OUT - Take authority over the demon spirits within you by issuing a command such as, "In the name of Jesus, I now take authority over every evil spirit present within me, and I command each and every one to submit to the authority invested in me by Jesus Christ!"

If you can address the demons by name (lust, anger, suicide, hate, fear, etc.), you will often find them submitting to your authority easier because it makes it harder on them to write you off as if you weren't talking to them. If somebody yelled "Hey, you!" in a crowd, you probably wouldn't pay any attention to them, but if they yelled out your name, you would be a lot quicker to respond. The same is true with demons:

if you address them by name, it is a lot easier to get their attention. Notice how many times Jesus addressed the demons by name, such as deaf and dumb spirits, etc.

Not every deliverance session requires you to refer to the demons by name, but it sure helps when you are able to get ahold of their names, like through remembering your previous involvement with evil spirits (if you accepted a spirit guide by the name of Daemon, then obviously Daemon needs to go). Another way to get the name is by the symptoms they are causing; for example, extreme guilt feelings are often caused by a spirit by the name of guilt, and other ways to get their names are by a word of knowledge from the Holy Spirit, or from the demons themselves (ask them for their name and listen for their response).

If I have a demon's name handy, I often like to use it. If not, I just proceed without it. Using your authority in Jesus, command the evil spirits (by name if possible) to come out of you in Jesus' name! Don't be alarmed if you find yourself throwing up all of a sudden, or coughing uncontrollably, screaming, etc. It's a good sign; it usually means they are on their way out! If you want to minimize manifestations, you can forbid them to manifest in Jesus' name. I usually like them to manifest, because it exposes them even more and somehow weakens their power and 'cocky attitude' when they are hauled out in the open where you can recognize them.

ENCOUNTERING GROUPINGS OF DEMONS - Demons often work in teams, and if you identify the strongman, it will help you figure out their game plan and give you a better idea of how to go about casting out certain demons first and unraveling their scheme. This is important, because this strongman is usually the big guy you are going after. Once you cast him out, the lesser demons usually follow suit much easier. However, sometimes it's better to cast out the lesser demons and then deal with their leader after they are all gone and he can no longer play games or hide behind them.

Since demons communicate with other demons both within and outside of you, I like to forbid and shut down their communication among each other. I like to issue a command like this: "I now shut down and forbid all lines of communication between the evil spirits within me, between themselves, and with those outside of me in Jesus' name!"

BINDING AND LOOSING - Binding is a temporary spiritual handcuffing. If you get worn out and need to continue a deliverance the next day, you could simply bind the remaining demons and continue the deliverance later on. Binding is also helpful when ministering to somebody else. You can bind and forbid the demons to interfere with the person as you work with them to tear down strongholds, break up legal grounds, etc.

Loosing refers to loosing a captive from a bondage. Jesus loosed the woman from a spirit of infirmity in Luke 13:12. You might say something like, "I loose myself from the spirit of fear in the name of Jesus! Spirit of fear, I command you to COME OUT in the name of Jesus!"

CHECKING TO SEE IF YOU ARE FREE - You should feel a noticeable relief when the demon(s) have left. However, they may just be hiding and trying to trick you into calling it a success, only to rear up their heads later on. Pray and ask the Holy Spirit to reveal to you if there are any demons remaining that need to be cast out, or whether the deliverance was successful. The long-term effect after a deliverance is usually your best indicator, but when there have been symptoms of the demon (such as fear, anger, suicidal urges, etc.), then I would expect those to be gone when the deliverance has been successful.

Don't forget to consider that in many cases, deliverance is a process and not just one session. If strongholds that the demons are hanging onto need to be torn down, they can usually take time as you tear them down. When the spirits leave you, though, you should feel the difference and be able to freely walk in your newfound freedom.

WARNING - I don't walk in constant fear of demons returning, but yet I also advise not to dabble in the things that opened you up to demons in the first place either. Keep your relationship with God cultivated, and don't let the enemy tempt you to let him back in.

If you are unsuccessful - Seek further knowledge on the ministry of deliverance and consider seeking the help of an experienced deliverance minister. Don't forget to consider that in many cases, deliverance is a process and not just one session. If strongholds that the demons are hanging onto need to be torn down, it can usually take time to tear them down. If you try your best and are getting nowhere, then I would seek help from an experienced minister.

HINDERANCES TO SUCCESSFUL DELIVERANCE

Not willing or ready - As elementary as this sounds, many deliverances are unsuccessful because the person was not ready or willing to be truly delivered. They were merely looking for a quick fix for their problem and were not willing to take the necessary steps to receive and maintain their deliverance.

Unforgiveness - Bitterness is a very popular source of spiritual defilement. Hebrews 12:14 says, "Pursue peace with all people, and holiness, without which no one will see the Lord." If you don't forgive others, God will not forgive you, as Matthew 6:15 confirms, "But if you do not forgive men their trespasses, neither will your Father forgive your trespasses." Unforgiveness puts us in the hands of tormenters which are demonic spirits.

Matthew 18:23–35, says, "Therefore the kingdom of heaven is like a certain king who wanted to settle accounts with his servant. And when he had begun to settle accounts, one was brought to him who owed him ten thousand talents. But as he was not able to pay, his master commanded that he be sold, with his wife and children and all that he had, and that payment be made. The servant therefore fell down before him, saying, 'Master, have patience with me, and I will pay you all.' Then the master of that servant was moved with compassion, released him, and forgave him the debt. But that servant went out and found one of his fellow servants who owed him a hundred denarii; and he laid hands on him and took him by the throat, saying, 'Pay me what you owe!' So his fellow servant fell down at his feet and begged him, saying, 'Have patience with me, and I will pay you all.' And he would not, but went and threw him into prison till he should pay the debt. So when his fellow servants saw what had been done, they were very grieved, and came and told their master all that had been done. Then his master, after he had called him, said to him, 'You wicked servant! I forgave you all that debt because you begged me. Should you not also have had compassion on your fellow servant, just as I had pity on you?' And his master was angry, and delivered him to the torturers until he should pay all that was due to him." So My heavenly Father also will do to you if each of you from his heart does not forgive his brother his trespasses.

Strongholds - Strongholds are incorrect thinking patterns in our minds in how we see things through. Many people see themselves as failures, so they feel like failures. Others see God as a cruel and dictating taskmaster, which causes them to feel distant and unloved by their heavenly Father. If you have a hard time feeling God's love, you can't cast out all the demons in the world, and if you don't see God as a loving God who loves you, it's going to be very difficult to feel and receive His love.

Unconfessed sins - If we confess and repent of our sins, God is faithful and just to forgive us (1 John 1:9: "If we confess our sins, He is faithful and just to forgive us our sins and to cleanse us from all unrighteousness."). But if we choose rather to keep our sins hidden to ourselves, we cannot expect God's forgiveness. There is also power in confessing our faults to one another, as James 5:16 tells us, "Confess your trespasses[a] to one another, and pray for one another, that you may be healed. The effective, fervent prayer of a righteous man avails much."

Soul ties - Having a soul tie with somebody means your soul is joined with theirs (1 Corinthians 6:16, "Or do you not know that he who is joined to a harlot is one body with her? For 'the two,' He says, 'shall become one flesh.'"). Being joined to another person with an unclean soul tie can allow the transference of spirits and bondage between the persons. It is vital to break of all bad soul ties from unhealthy past relationships so that the enemy cannot use them against us.

Cursed objects - The Bible gives us a clear pattern of destroying false gods, idols, and so-called cursed objects. God warns us that bringing a cursed object into our home can bring a curse upon us as well (Deuteronomy 7:26: "Nor shall you bring an abomination into your house, lest you be doomed to destruction like it. You shall utterly detest it and utterly abhor it, for it is an accursed thing.").

Lack of faith - Not understanding or believing God's will or the truth about your situation can keep you in bondage as well. If you don't realize the authority and freedom you have in Christ, it can be very hard to walk in it and eat of its fruit. Knowledge of the truth is indeed an important tool in our spiritual toolkit.

Unrenounced vows - Vows and oaths bind the soul (Numbers 30:2: "If a man makes a vow to the LORD, or swears an oath to bind himself by some agreement, he shall not break his word; he shall do according to all that proceeds out of his mouth."). The way to break free from any ungodly vows is to repent of it and renounce it verbally in Jesus' name.

Unbroken curses - Both ancestral curses and curses encountered in one's own life must be broken. I believe ancestral sin curses are automatically broken so long as we have accepted Christ, and do not take part in our ancestor's wickedness, but other types of curses must be broken before complete deliverance can be obtained and kept.

Residing spirits - Demons often need to be cast out of a person before they are able to fully overcome many persistent bondages. Demons are often found behind many issues such as fear, depression, physical infirmities (arthritis, cancer, deafness, etc.), mental illnesses, etc., and need to be driven out as Jesus and the early church went about doing.

THE IMPORTANCE OF SELF-FORGIVENESS FOR SUCESSFUL DELIVERANCE

If you look in the mirror and look yourself in the eyes but you don't like the person you see, then you need to forgive yourself and learn how to love the person that God has made in you! This is what we call a stronghold, or an incorrect thinking pattern that needs to be torn down in your mind. If you have repented of your sins and taken them before the Lord, then you are forgiven ... and now you need to comc to rcalizc the power of that. You need to stop associating your failures with your "new creation" image, for God's Word says...

2 Corinthians 5:17 says, "Therefore, if anyone is in Christ, he is a new creation; old things have passed away; behold, all things have become new."

Can you honestly look in the mirror and tell yourself "I love you" and mean it with your heart? I'm not talking about a prideful way, but a humble means of accepting who God has formed in you. We need to love and accept the person that Christ has made in us and forgive ourselves as Christ has forgiven us!

The importance of forgiving yourself

When you look inside you hate yourself, and you could kick yourself over and over for your past failures and choices. You've come to Jesus and repented, but you haven't really accepted the truth about what Jesus has done for you yet. You still feel ashamed and guilty over your past and you keep holding it against yourself. *The way you see yourself is not an accurate picture of what Christ has done for you. It is basically denying the work that Jesus accomplished for you on the cross!* If your sins are forgiven, then you need to see yourself as separated from your sins ... but no, the enemy will try diligently to remind you of your past and continue to beat you up over sins that were supposed to be nailed to the cross. You are wrapped up in guilt and condemnation, my friend ... and you NEED to forgive yourself. You can go through deliverance, but if you don't forgive yourself for the mistakes you've made, you won't experience the breakthrough that you need to be totally set free.

When the recipient of a gift receives it gladly and with joy, the giver is glorified. But when the recipient receives the gift but ignores it, the giver is mocked, belittled, and feels unappreciated. When we fail to forgive ourselves, we are like a child who is given a trip to Disney World for Christmas, yet he keeps complaining that he can't go ... even after his parents have already packed the car and are waiting on him to get in! How would you feel if you were that child's parents? Wouldn't you feel sick inside knowing you spend all that money on this trip, the tickets, the hotel reservations, etc., and your son refuses to go because he doesn't believe that what you gave him was real? Think how your heavenly Father feels when He looks down and sees His children walking around beating themselves up over things that He shed His blood so they could be forgiven and set free from?

I believe it is clear that failing to forgive ourselves from our past mistakes is denying the work of the cross and the shed Blood of Christ in our lives. When God's Word tells us that we've been washed clean with the Blood of Christ and our sins are removed through the atoning work that Jesus did for us ... yet we still "could kick ourselves" for our mistakes, then we are basically saying, "I don't care what the Blood of Jesus has done, I still hate myself for what I've done!" It's staggering to think such a thing, but that is what really happens when we refuse to forgive ourselves.

If you don't see yourself as a new creature in Christ, then *you have a serious problem*. You will be hindered and held back from freely and confidently living out who you really are in Christ! You will be hesitant and feel unworthy to approach your Heavenly Father, because you feel you're a failure and unworthy ... this is why it is vital for your conscience to be cleansed of dead works (your past failures)...

Hebrews 9:14 states, "How much more shall the blood of Christ, who through the eternal Spirit offered Himself without spot to God, *purge your conscience from dead works to serve the living God?*"

Failing to forgive yourself will put blinders on your spiritual eyesight quickly. It will cause you to see things through the eyes of guilt, shame, and condemnation. It will ruin your faith and cause you to go blind spiritually:

2 Peter 1:9 explains: "For he who lacks these things is shortsighted, even to blindness, and has forgotten that he was cleansed from his old sins."

In the following verse, we are told to forgive one another, but did you know that the root word for the phrase "one another" actually includes yourself? The Greek root word *heautou* refers not only to others, but also to ourselves!

Colossians 3:13 says, "Bearing with one another, and forgiving one another, if anyone has a complaint against another; even as Christ forgave you, so you also must do."

Unforgiveness is a known door opener to torment from demonic spirits. Matthew 18:23–35 tells us how the unforgiving person is turned over into the hands of tormenters (that is, tormenting spirits). If we are unforgiving towards ourselves, we open the door for tormenting spirits to come against us because we are not really accepting the work that Christ did for us on the cross. Another key to the demonic is bitterness, and when we become bitter with ourselves, we become defiled spiritually:

Hebrews 12:15 says, "Looking carefully lest anyone fall short of the grace of God; lest any root of bitterness springing up cause trouble, and by this many become defiled."

God's Word tells us that Jesus purged (that is, removed) our sin (Hebrews 1:3: "Who being the brightness of His glory and the express image of His person, and upholding all things by the word of His power, when He had by Himself purged our sins, sat down at the right hand of the Majesty on high"; "...when he had by himself purged our sins...," but if we fail to forgive ourselves, we are in essence calling God's Word a liar! We are saying, "I hate myself because I did that sin ... I won't forgive myself of it!" When God's Word tells us that the sin has been PURGED or REMOVED from us ... who are we to say that it is still part of our past? We are in essence calling God's Word a LIE!

I can't tell you how important it is to realize that when the recipient of a gift (you and I) receives a gift (of Jesus' shed blood for the forgiveness of our sins) with joy and enjoys it to the fullness, the giver of that gift (that is Jesus) is glorified! Failing to forgive ourselves is denying or rejecting the gift of God and brings no glory (actually dishonor and humiliation) to what Jesus did for us.

What Hebrews chapter ten has to say...
Animal Sacrifices Insufficient

“10 For the law, having a shadow of the good things to
come, and not the very image of the things, can never with
these same sacrifices, which they offer continually year by
year, make those who approach perfect. 2 For then would
they not have ceased to be offered? For the worshipers, once
purified, would have had no more consciousness of sins.
3 But in those sacrifices there is a reminder of sins every
year. 4 For it is not possible that the blood of bulls and goats
could take away sins.”

Christ’s Death Fulfills God’s Will

“5 Therefore, when He came into the world, He said:
‘Sacrifice and offering You did not desire, But a body You
have prepared for Me. 6 In burnt offerings and sacrifices for
sin You had no pleasure.’ 7 Then I said, ‘Behold, I have
come—In the volume of the book it is written of Me—To do
Your will, O God.’ 8 Previously saying, ‘Sacrifice and
offering, burnt offerings, and offerings for sin You did not
desire, nor had pleasure in them’ (which are offered
according to the law), 9 then He said, ‘Behold, I have come
to do Your will, O God.’ He takes away the first that He
may establish the second. 10 By that will we have been
sanctified through the offering of the body of Jesus Christ
once for all.

Christ's Death Perfects the Sanctified

"[11] And every priest stands ministering daily and offering repeatedly the same sacrifices, which can never take away sins. [12] But this Man, after He had offered one sacrifice for sins forever, sat down at the right hand of God, [13] from that time waiting till His enemies are made His footstool. [14] For by one offering He has perfected forever those who are being sanctified. [15] But the Holy Spirit also witnesses to us; for after He had said before, [16] "This is the covenant that I will make with them after those days, says the LORD: I will put My laws into their hearts, and in their minds I will write them," [17] then He adds, "Their sins and their lawless deeds I will remember no more." [18] Now where there is remission of these, there is no longer an offering for sin.

Hold Fast Your Confession

"[19] Therefore, brethren, having boldness to enter the Holiest by the blood of Jesus, [20] by a new and living way which He consecrated for us, through the veil, that is, His flesh, [21] and having a High Priest over the house of God, [22] let us draw near with a true heart in full assurance of faith, having our hearts sprinkled from an evil conscience and our bodies washed with pure water. [23] Let us hold fast the confession of our hope without wavering, for He who promised is faithful. [24] And let us consider one another in order to stir up love and good works, [25] not forsaking the assembling of ourselves together, as is the manner of some, but exhorting one another, and so much the more as you see the Day approaching."

RESTORATION PROCESS DURING AND AFTER DELIVERANCE

Be honest to yourself

Realize that deep down inside, you're not happy with the person of your past. If you are in denial, then forget trying to treat the root of your problem. You need to see the problem before you can apply the solution. It might even be helpful to list all the things that you hate about your past and one-by-one give them to the Lord and release yourself from each failure.

You need to realize that your debt has been PAID

The only way you can beat yourself up after Jesus has paid your debt is if you aren't accepting the gift that He has given you. If He's paid the debt and you keep denying that fact, then you are rejecting the very gift that God has given you! You need to accept what Jesus has done for you by faith.

Galatians 2:16 says, "Knowing that a man is not justified by the works of the law but by the faith of

Jesus Christ, even we have believed in Christ Jesus, that we might be justified by the faith in Christ and not by the works of the law; for by the works of the law shall no flesh be justified."

The blood of Jesus was shed for the payment of your sins: Matthew 26:28 explains, "For this is My blood of the new covenant, which is shed for many for the remission of sins.." Because of the powerful work that Christ did for us on the cross, God's Word tells us to come boldly unto the throne of grace, so that we can obtain mercy: Hebrews 4:16 confirms, "Let us therefore come boldly to the throne of grace that we may obtain mercy and find grace to help in time of need."

The price for your redemption has been paid in full. It's up to you to receive it and realize that the blood of Jesus actually removes the sin from your record. Now you need to see yourself as being forgiven and justified (which means, "just as if you've never sinned"). In Luke 7, Jesus took a very sinful woman (likely a prostitute) and freely washed her clean without hesitation...

Luke 7:47: "Therefore I say to you, Her sins, which are many, are forgiven, for she loved much. But to whom little is forgiven, the same loves little."

The above verse is just one example of how freely Jesus would forgive a person of their sins. It is true that if we take our sin to Jesus, He will freely forgive us without hesitation: Romans 3:24 confirms thus, “Being justified freely by His grace through the redemption that is in Christ Jesus.”

There is no sin that you can take to Jesus that He will not forgive … for the Bible tells us that He is prepared to cleanse us of ALL unrighteousness if we will turn to Him with our failures! 1 John 1:9 states, “If we confess our sins, He is faithful and just to forgive us our sins and to cleanse us from all unrighteousness.”

Allow the Holy Spirit to heal your soul

You need to let God heal you; as long as you keep holding something against yourself, you are blocking the Holy Spirit’s power from entering and healing that area of your mind and life! You need to open up your heart and allow the light of Christ to shine into the darkness of your soul.

Begin to see the “new creature” of Christ within you

You are not seeing yourself as you really are. If you’ve repented of your past and sought God’s forgiveness, then you are forgiven or justified (which means “just as if I’ve never sinned”). It’s not that you should try to forget what happened (don’t remind yourself of it either, though), but the key is to see your past through the Blood of Jesus. You need to see your past as “paid in full” by the work that Christ did for you on the cross! Seeing things with this perspective changes everything! *You need to begin seeing yourself through the blood of Jesus.*

One day when the enemy was trying to beat me up over my past, the Holy Spirit spoke clearly to me and said, "You need to KNOW that you're clean ... *your faith depends upon it*!"

Some Bible verses to meditate on

I encourage you to repeat these scriptures out loud, for there is indeed power in the spoken confession of God's truth. Do this on a regular (daily) basis and it will begin to renew your mind according to the truth found in God's Word.

2 Corinthians 5:17: "Therefore, if anyone is in Christ, he is a new creation; old things have passed away; behold, all things have become new."

Say to yourself, "I am a new creation in Christ; old things have passed away and all things become new."

1 John 1:9: "If we confess our sins, He is faithful and just to forgive us our sins and to cleanse us from all unrighteousness."

Say to yourself, "When I confess my sin, He is faithful and just and will forgive me it, regardless what kind of unrighteousness I may have committed."

Colossians 3:13: "Bearing with one another, and forgiving one another, if anyone has a complaint against another; even as Christ forgave you, so you also must do."

Say to yourself, "I will love and forgive myself, as Christ has forgiven me."

Psalms 103:12: "As far as the east is from the west, So far has He removed our transgressions from us."

Say to yourself, "My sins are not simply covered, but they are removed from me ... taken so far from me that there is no way they can be considered part of me anymore!"

Revelations 1:5: "And from Jesus Christ, the faithful witness, the firstborn from the dead, and the ruler over the kings of the earth. To Him who loved us and washed[a] us from our sins in His own blood,

Say to yourself, "I am washed from my sins by the Blood of Christ Jesus Himself."

Matthew 26:28: "For this is My blood of the new covenant, which is shed for many for the remission of sins." (The NT Greek tells us that the word 'remission' here means, "Forgiveness or pardon, of sins (letting them go as if they had never been committed), remission of the penalty.")

Say to yourself, "Because the Blood of Christ was shed for me, I am let go as if I have never sinned."

Romans 5:1: “Therefore, having been justified by faith, we have peace with God through our Lord Jesus Christ.”

Say to yourself, “I have been justified (made right, as if I have never sinned) by faith and have peace with God through my Lord Jesus Christ.”

Galatians 2:16: “Knowing that a man is not justified by the works of the law but by faith in Jesus Christ, even we have believed in Christ Jesus, that we might be justified by faith in Christ and not by the works of the law; for by the works of the law no flesh shall be justified.”

Say to yourself, “I cannot be justified by works of the law or acts of righteousness, but by my faith in Christ Jesus.”

Romans 3:22: “Even the righteousness of God, through faith in Jesus Christ, to all and on all who believe. For there is no difference.”

Say to yourself, “Because I believe, the righteousness of God is upon me.”

Romans 4:3–8: “For what does the Scripture say? ‘Abraham believed God, and it was accounted to him for righteousness.’ Now to him who works, the wages are not counted as grace but as debt. But to him who does not work but believes on Him who justifies the ungodly, his faith is accounted for righteousness, just as David also describes the blessedness of the man to whom God imputes righteousness apart from works: Blessed are those whose lawless deeds are forgiven, And whose sins are covered; Blessed is the man to whom the LORD shall not impute sin."

Say to yourself, "The righteousness of God is upon me, not as a result of works of the law, but through faith in Christ Jesus and the grace of God. I did not earn it, yet He gave it to me, and I receive it by faith in Christ Jesus."

Galatians 2:20: "I have been crucified with Christ; it is no longer I who live but Christ lives in me; and the life which I now live in the flesh I live by faith in the Son of God, who loved me and gave Himself for me."

Say to yourself, "The old me has been crucified and my old man has been buried with Christ. Now my life is in Christ as I have been raised to life with Him and I am free to walk in the newness of life."

Isaiah 43:25: "I, even I, am He who blots out your transgressions for My own sake; And I will not remember your sins.

I, even I, am he that blotted out thy transgressions for mine own sake, and will not remember thy sins."

Say to yourself, "My Heavenly Father chose to forget my past sins for HIS sake. When He looks at me, He doesn't want to see my sin ... He wants to see His precious creation who was purchased and justified with the Blood of His Son Jesus Christ."

Hebrews 9:14: "How much more shall the blood of Christ, who through the eternal Spirit offered Himself without spot to God, cleanse your conscience from dead works to serve the living God?"

Say to yourself, "Because of the Blood of Christ, my conscience can be purged of dead works (your past failures) so that I can serve the Living God."

Hebrews 10:22: "Let us draw near with a true heart in full assurance of faith, having our hearts sprinkled from an evil conscience and our bodies washed with pure water."

Say to yourself, "Not only did God choose to forget my sins, but He also wants me to forget them as well. He wants me to draw near to Him with a true heart, in full assurance of faith, being sprinkled clean from an evil conscience."

Romans 8:1: "There is therefore now no condemnation to those who are in Christ Jesus, who do not walk according to the flesh, but according to the Spirit."

Say to yourself, "I am in Christ Jesus, and therefore free from condemnation."

Failing to see yourself as God's Word sees you denying the very work that Jesus did for us when He suffered and died on our behalf. Don't let this continue in your life another day ... accept the free gift of God and begin to see yourself as a new creation in Christ

Jesus whose past failures have been purchased with the precious Blood of Jesus!

If you hate the person that you are but God's Word tells us that you are a new creation who's been washed clean with the Blood of Christ, whose "past" has been purchased with the work that Christ did for us on the cross ... do you still hate that person? Do you hate the new creation that God has made you? Or are you still a sinner in need of salvation? Are you in Christ or not?

Romans 8:1: "There is therefore now no condemnation to them which are in Christ Jesus, who walk not after the flesh, but after the Spirit."

Do you want to bring glory and honor to Jesus? Then accept His gift with great joy and begin to see yourself as that new creation ... begin to see your past failures as being "paid in full" by the great sacrifice that Christ made for you. Begin to see yourself the same way that your Heavenly Father sees you!

DELIVERANCE QUESTIONNAIRE

Each and every question does not necessarily indicate bondage, but will help give a clearer picture of your deliverance and can be helpful in locating obvious bondages in your life. These questions can reveal strongholds, demonic bondages, and legal grounds that may need to be addressed.

Part I: The bondage

1. When did this bondage start?

____

____

____

____

____

2. Were there any unusual things that took place (or you did) when this bondage started?

____

____

____

____

____

3. If this bondage started when you were a child: Do you have ancestors who have suffered from a similar kind of bondage?

____

____

____

____

____

4. What kind of bondage are you facing? (fears, depression, voices in your mind, mental illness, physical illness, mental torment, spiritual torment, etc.. Please be as detailed as possible.

____

____

____

____

____

5. What are the things that have impacted your life? (parent's death, trauma, a certain situation that changed your life, anything that 'changed' you.)

____

____

____

____

____

Part II: Your ancestor's background

1. Do you have ancestors who have struggled with similar problems or bondages?

____

____

____

____

____

2. Did your bondage start as a child and appear to have no reason to be there?

____

____

____

____

____

3. Do you have siblings who suffer from similar bondages or oppression?

____

____

____

____

____

Part III: Soul ties

1. Have you been involved with extramarital sex? Are you attracted to an ex-lover? Is he or she a good/godly influence for you?

____

____

____

____

____

2. Have you been divorced?

____

____

____

____

____

3. Do you feel an unusual attraction to a past boyfriend, girlfriend or lover (who is obviously not right for you)?

____

____

____

____

____

4. Do you let anybody dominate, control, or make your choices for you?

____

____

____

____

____

5. Have you ever formed a blood covenant (blood brothers, etc.) with another person?

____

____

____

____

____

6. Have you ever made vows or agreements with somebody in order to strengthen the relationship or commit yourself to each other?

____

____

____

____

____

7. Do you see any ungodly relationships in your past where gifts were exchanged? (Are you holding onto something that was given to you from somebody you had adultery with, etc.)

____

____

____

8. Have you ever had ungodly relations with an animal?

9. Do you have in your possession any pictures of somebody whom you may have an ungodly soul tie with? (A picture of you with somebody you had an adultery with, etc.)

Part IV: Relationship with parents

1. What do you think of your parents?

____

____

____

____

____

2. How would you explain your childhood?

____

____

____

____

____

3. Were you close to your parents while growing up? If not, why?

____

____

____

____

____

4. How would you explain your relationship with your parents? Was it good, bad, or very cold?

____

____

____

____

____

5. Did you feel rejection from your parents?

____

____

____

____

____

6. Was either of your parents overly passive or controlling?

____

____

____

____

____

7. Has either of your parents been divorced? Remarried? Are your parents divorced?

____

____

____

____

____

8. How would you describe your relationship with your siblings growing up?

____

____

____

____

____

Part V: Rejection and abuse

1. Were your parents married when you were conceived? Were you the right sex? Did your parents not want you, or want you to be different (gender, etc.) in any way? If so, explain.

____

____

____

____

____

2. Did you feel rejected as a child? As an adult? If so, by whom? Explain.

____

____

____

____

____

3. Did you face abuse? What kind (emotional, physical, sexual, etc.) and by whom?

____

____

____

____

____

4. Have you faced rejection from your peers, classmates, friends, or those around you?

____

____

____

____

____

5. Have you ever been put down, belittled, or made fun of? If so, by whom? Explain.

____

____

____

____

____

6. If you have faced rejection or abuse, how did you respond? Do you feel you are still paying a price for it? If so, how?

____

____

____

____

____

7. How do you respond to rejection right now?

____

____

____

____

____

8. Do you reject yourself (self-rejection)? If so, why and in what ways?

____

____

____

____

____

Part VI: Unforgiveness or bitterness

1. Is there anybody you feel edgy around with? (Don't like them, feel anything in your heart against them, etc.)

____

____

____

____

____

2. Do you have anything against anybody? In other words, is there anybody you have a hard time demonstrating the love of Christ to?

____

____

____

____

____

3. Has anybody wronged you that you haven't forgiven from your heart (thoughts, feelings, emotions, etc.)?

____

____

____

____

____

4. How do your view your siblings, parents, coworkers, etc.? Do you have any hard feelings against them?

____

____

____

____

____

5. Do you make a habit of blaming yourself for everything? Do you obsess over your mistakes and feel unusually guilty for them?

____

____

____

____

____

6. Do you deeply regret things that you've done in your past? Could you kick yourself over something you've done in your past? If so, explain.

____

____

____

____

____

Part VII: Personality

1. Are you a very positive or negative person?

____

____

____

____

____

2. Do you feel confident in yourself? If so, why?

____

____

____

____

____

3. Do you have a low self-esteem? If so, why?

____

____

____

____

____

4. Are you domineering or controlling? If so, to whom, and in what ways? Why?

____

____

____

____

____

5. Are you an achiever (a go-getter)? If so, in what ways?

____

____

____

____

____

6. Do you feel you are always right and that if everybody did everything your way, this world would be a better place to live?

____

____

____

____

____

7. How do you treat your children? Husband? Are you controlling, passive, etc.?

____

____

____

____

____

____

8. Do you like people to 'look at you' (as in receive attention)?

____

____

____

____

____

Part VIII: Emotional health

1. Do you strive to feel accepted? If so, how does this affect your lifestyle? By whom do you want to feel accepted?

____

____

____

____

____

2. Are you always stressed out? If so, why?

____

____

____

____

____

3. Do you feel hurt? If so, by whom/what and why?

____

____

____

____

____

4. Do you feel good about yourself? If not, why?

____

____

____

____

____

____

5. Do you feel depressed? If so, why? When did it start? Did your parents or grandparents struggle with depression? If so, then do you know when it started and why? Do you have siblings who are also struggling? Do you feel your depression is rational or irrational?

____

____

____

____

____

6. Do you struggle with fears (fear of heights, dying, being hopeless, failure, never marrying, etc.)? If so, what is it that you fear?

____

____

____

____

____

7. Do you worry about things? What things do you worry about? Why?

____

____

____

____

____

8. Do you struggle with anger? Do you have a short temper?

____

____

____

____

____

9. Do you have any insecurities? If so, explain.

____

____

____

____

____

10. Do you feel any self-pity or feel sorry for yourself? Have you ever felt this? If so, why?

____

____

____

____

____

11. Do you find it easy to hate people? If so, over what kind of things would a person have to do to make you hate them?

____

____

____

____

____

12. Do you have any irrational feelings? If so, what are they?

____

____

____

____

____

13. Do you feel like something is wrong with you?

14. Do you feel excessively guilty over anything? Is this a continual problem?

____

____

____

____

____

15. Are you very confused and forgetful (i.e., beyond normal)?

____

____

____

____

____

16. Are you aware of any emotional wounds that have affected you?

____

____

____

____

____

17. Have you ever been deeply embarrassed over something? What was it?

____

____

____

____

____

18. Have you been in or are currently experiencing very difficult (depressing) circumstances which may cause you to feel hopeless or depressed?

____

____

____

____

____

Part IX: Who are you in Christ? And how do you see God?

1. How do you explain your relationship with God?

____

____

____

____

____

2. Do you feel you aren't good enough to meet His standards?

____

____

____

____

____

3. Do you see Him as a loving father, or a dictator?

____

____

____

____

____

4. Do you believe that it's only by the Blood of Jesus that your sins are forgiven? Or do you feel you need to earn your forgiveness in any way?

____

____

____

____

____

5. Do you feel God's love in your life?

____

____

____

____

____

6. Do you feel like your sins are forgiven? Or do you feel guilty?

____

____

____

____

____

7. Do you feel excessively guilty in everyday life?

____

____

____

____

____

8. Do you feel that by doing good things, you earn God's love and acceptance?

____

____

____

____

____

9. Do you feel that God is angry or upset with you?

____

____

____

____

____

Part X: Spoken curses, vows & oaths

1. Have you ever spoken something negative about yourself that has come to pass? For example: "I'm sick and tired...," or "If I don't quit typing, I'm going to get arthritis!"

____

____

____

____

____

2. Have your parents, or those in authority over you spoken out a curse over you? For example: "You'll never amount to anything!" or "You'll never get out of debt," or "You're so dumb"?

____

____

____

____

____

3. Have you ever made a vow out of anger? If so, what? For example: "I'll never let anybody push me

around again!" or "I'm never going to be hurt again!"

____

____

____

____

____

4. Have you ever wished to die? Have you ever said it?

____

____

____

____

____

5. If you have made any vows or oaths, what are they?

____

____

____

____

____

Part XI: Relationships

1. Do you have many friends? What kind of people are they?

____

____

____

____

____

2. Do you have a hard time trying to meet new people or make friends?

____

____

____

____

____

3. Are you socially outgoing or shy? If so, why?

____

____

____

____

____

4. How would you define your relationship with your spouse?

____

____

____

____

____

Part XII: Sexuality

1. Have you ever had unholy sex (fornication, adultery, sodomy, bestiality, with a child, etc.)? What kind?

____

____

____

____

____

2. Have you struggled with lust, fantasy, or unholy sexual thoughts? If so, what kind?

____

____

____

____

____

3. Have you been attracted to pornography?

____

____

____

____

____

4. Do you have homosexual thoughts and desires? If so, have you acted upon those feelings?

____

____

____

____

____

5. How do you feel about your sexuality? (Do you feel dirty about it, or do you feel it's a wonderful blessing that God's given you?)

____

____

____

____

____

6. Do you withhold sex from your spouse or are you fidgety? Do you enjoy a healthy relationship with your spouse sexually? How does he or she react?

____

____

____

____

____

7. Have you ever been raped or sexually abused?

____

____

____

____

____

8. Have you ever woke up and felt a sexual presence with you? There are demons that imitate male and female functions, and stimulate their host (a person) sexually (beyond the normal 'wet dream').

____

____

____

____

____

9. Do you struggle or have you struggled with masturbation?

____

____

____

____

____

10. Do you struggle or have you struggled with any other sexually related thoughts, desires, or bondages?

____

____

____

____

____

11. Is there anything sexually that you are ashamed of?

____

____

____

____

____

Part XIII: Addictions

1. Do you have any addictions (drugs, alcohol, smoking, eating, sex, TV, etc.)? If so, what kind? When did they start?

____

____

____

____

____

2. Did anybody else in your family (siblings, ancestors, etc.) struggle with any addictions? If so, what? Who?

____

____

____

____

____

3. Have you ever had, or currently have, any sort of obsession over anything? If so, what?

____

____

____

____

____

Part XIV: False religions

Examples of false religions: Buddhism, Hindu, Jehovah's Witness, Mormonism, Christian Scientists, eastern religions, etc.

1. Have you ever been involved with any false religions? If so, why, when, and how long? How do you feel about those beliefs now?

____

____

____

____

____

2. Have you ever been involved in any secret societies such as Freemasonry? If so, how deep were you involved?

____

____

____

____

____

Part XV: The occult and Satanism

1. Have you ever shown interest in the occult? If so, in what ways? (Read up on it, dabbled in it, etc.)

____

____

____

____

____

2. Do you still feel drawn or attracted to the occult?

____

____

____

____

____

3. Have you had any interest in horror or thriller style movies or novels? Are you still attracted to these things?

____

____

____

____

____

4. Have you ever made a vow with the devil? If so, what?

____

____

____

____

____

5. Married Satan?

____

____

____

____

____

6. Worshipped a demon or Satan?

____

____

____

____

____

7. Have you ever put a curse or spell on somebody?

____

____

____

____

____

8. Are you aware of any curses or spells placed on you? If so, what? Who did it?

____

____

____

____

____

9. Dabbled with an Ouija board? If so, why?

____

____

____

____

____

10. Ever been a member of a coven (group of thirteen witches)? Explain.

____

____

____

____

____

11. Communicated with the dead? Explain.

____

____

____

____

____

12. Told somebody's fortune or went to see a fortune teller? Explain.

____

____

____

____

____

13. Ever read your horoscope?

____

____

____

____

____

14. Watched or been involved in demonic worship? Explain.

____

____

____

____

____

15. Been involved with, or a victim of, Satanic ritual abuse? Explain.

____

____

____

____

____

16. Been baptized into a false religion or any other evil baptism? If so, what were you baptized into? When?

____

____

____

____

____

17. Have you ever had a spirit guide?

____

____

____

____

____

18. Have you ever been involved with meditation, yoga, karate, or related activities?

____

____

____

____

____

19. Were you or anybody in your family superstitious? If so, who?

____

____

____

____

____

20. Ever been involved in astral (out of body) travel?

____

____

____

____

____

21. If you have made any vows or oaths, what are they? Were there any sacrifices or rituals that accompanied them?

____

____

____

____

____

22. Have you ever made a blood pact before? If so, with whom (including persons, demons, and Satan) and for what purpose?

____

____

____

____

____

23. Have you ever partaken in automatic writing, automatic drawing, or automatic painting?

____

____

____

____

____

24. Have you ever been involved in Yoga, transcendental meditation, or similar activities?

____

____

____

____

____

25. Have you ever sought healing from a spiritual source other than Jesus Christ? (New Age healing, energy healing, etc.)

____

____

____

____

____

26. Any other involvement in the occult? Explain.

____

____

____

____

____

Part XVI: Unconfessed sins

1. Are there any un-confessed sins that you have not repented of? (Usually something you've done, that you know is wrong, but won't admit to it. An abortion, stealing, etc. are some examples.)

____

____

____

____

____

2. Is there anything you've been hiding inside that you haven't confessed?

____

____

____

____

____

3. Do you feel excessively guilty over something(s) you've done in the past? If so, what?

____

____

____

____

____

Part XVII: Cursed objects

1. Do you have any idols, occult rings, or anything that could hold evil spiritual value in your home? If so, what? Any objects that hold evil spiritual value must be destroyed.

____

____

____

____

____

2. Do you have any gifts saved from sinful relationships? If so, explain. For example, if a man gives a woman a personal gift during an adultery, the gift needs to be sold or destroyed.

____

____

____

____

____

Part XVIII: Severe trauma, abuse, and disassociation

1. Have you ever been exposed to extreme abuse or a traumatic experience? Did it have a drastic effect on your emotional or mental system? If so, what happened? How did it affect you?

____

____

____

____

____

2. Have you ever disassociated or been diagnosed with Dissociative Identity Disorder (DID) or Multiple Personality Disorder (MPD)?

____

____

____

____

____

3. Are you aware of any alters (other personalities) that you may have? (If so, tell me about them.)

____

____

____

____

____

4. Do you have a memory gap where you cannot remember a certain time of your life?

____

____

____

____

____

5. Do you have false memories of things that really didn't take place?

____

____

____

____

____

6. Have you ever been in a car accident or other traumatic situation? Have you ever witnessed a tragedy in real life?

____

____

____

____

____

Part XIX: Weaknesses

1. Do you struggle with any habitual sins? If so, what? Do you want to break those bad habits?

____

____

____

____

____

2. Do you struggle with any weaknesses such as lust, anger, hate, etc.? If so, what? Do you know where they came from or how they got started? Do you want to break free from those weaknesses?

____

____

____

____

____

Part XX: Pregnancy issues

1. Have you ever said something along the lines of, "I will never have children"?

____

____

____

____

____

2. Have you ever had an abortion or attempted one?

____

____

____

____

____

3. Have you ever had incest or ungodly sexual relations with somebody related to you? (See Leviticus 20:19–21, as this can cause a curse to land upon you which needs to be broken)

____

____

____

____

____

Part XXI: Other things to look for

1. Have you ever tried drugs? If so, how much, and how did it affect you? Why did you try drugs?

____

____

____

____

____

2. Have you ever thought about or attempted suicide?

____

____

____

____

____

3. Do you have any physical or mental disabilities, diseases or illnesses? Explain.

____

____

____

____

____

4. Do you want, and are willing, to be delivered? Are you willing to give up those demon spirits and maybe make some lifestyle changes in order to keep your deliverance?

____

____

____

____

____

5. Do you experience unusual confusion settle upon you as you try to pray and read the Bible?

____

____

____

____

____

6. What kind of music do you like? (Please list all styles of music you currently enjoy, and give examples in each category you list, such as some names of artists and songs.)

____

____

____

____

7. Have you previously enjoyed hard rock, metal, acid, alternative, rap, New Age, or any other kind of worldly music? (Please provide some examples of artists and songs from each genre (type/style) of music you list.)

____

____

____

____

____

8. Have you had any nightmares or weird experiences at night while supposedly sleeping?

____

____

____

____

____

9. Have you ever been in a trance or had an out-of-body experience?

____

____

____

____

____

10. Have you ever noticed time slipped right out from under you? For example, you look at your watch and it's 7:00 PM, then you look again what seemed like 15 minutes later and it's 2:00 AM. This is a sign of a trance.

____

____

____

____

____

11. Have you ever touched or kissed a dead body? If so, explain whom and why and what happened afterwards.

____

____

____

____

____

12. Do you feel that you somehow have to earn your forgiveness? Do you 'wonder' if your sins are truly forgiven—all of them? Are you aware of any signs of legalism or religious spirits operating in your mind?

____

____

____

____

____

13. Do you have any physical infirmities, sickness or diseases? If so, please list them.

____

____

____

____

____

14. Are you on any medications? If so, please explain.

____

____

____

15. Are you entertained by movies or TV shows that glorify death, murder, pain or suffering of others? Please explain.

16. Have you ever had any other kind of weird encounter with the spiritual realm?

PRAYER FOR SALVATION

Pray the following to receive Jesus Christ as Your Savior

Dear heavenly Father, I come to you in the name of Jesus. I acknowledge to You that I am a sinner, and I am sorry for my sins and the life that I have lived; I need Your forgiveness.

I believe that Your only begotten Son Jesus Christ shed His precious blood on the cross at Calvary and died for my sins, and I am now willing to turn from my sin.

You said in Your Holy Word, Romans 10:9, that if we confess the Lord our God and believe in our hearts that God raised Jesus from the dead, we shall be saved.

Right now I confess Jesus as the Lord of my soul. With my heart, I believe that God raised Jesus from the dead. This very moment I accept Jesus Christ as my own personal Savior and according to His Word, right now I am saved.

Thank you, Jesus, for Your unlimited grace that has saved me from my sins. I thank You Jesus that your grace never leads to license, but rather it always leads to repentance. Therefore, Lord Jesus, transform my life so I may bring glory and honor to You alone and not to myself.

PRAYER FOR HEALING

Dear Lord, You are the Just Judge, Holy and True. You are the Most High God. You give us life. You hold all power in Your hands. You are the Mighty One from God who carries the world, and is ruler over all the earth.

You, oh Most Blessed One are the Giver of Life. In You are only good things. In You is mercy and love. In You is healing of the nations. In You is freedom of worry and freedom of pain. Lord Almighty, You loved us so much. You were sent from Your Father, sent to save us from destruction. We truly can never make it to Heaven without the help of Jesus the Son, who was sent to earth to help us. You, Lord are full of mercy and grace, please forgive us for our faults. Lord Jesus, in You all healing is performed.

You, Lord, are the miracle worker. In Your Spirit, Your gift of healing is alive. In You Lord we can put our trust that You can heal us, and protect us from the enemy, and death of our soul. You, Lord, are miracle worker for the sick, and for the lost souls. You, Lord, forgive us and save us from condemnation. You cleanse us and make us born again new. You give us a clean heart full of peace. You, Lord, are the Light. In You is all truth. Your way, Lord, is the way to Heavenly Hope. Your hands, Lord, created the universe.

You, Lord, are the true Giver of Life. Every child is a miracle of Life. Life rests in Your Hands. Wrap us as a close-knit family, draw us near to you, Lord, and bind us with your Loving Hands. Let us be drawn closer to You. You are the Vine, dear Lord, and we are the branches.

You carry all knowledge and all power. You, Lord,[are our medicine. Your Words, Lord, are Truth and Life. Help us put our trust in You. You, Lord, are the greatest physician. You heal, You protect, You care, You love, You are kind, You are patient, You are thoughtful, You are strength.

You, Lord, are our Creator. You know our thoughts, our sighings and our cryings and every hair on our head. You are Wonderful and make all good things for us. Heal us, Lord, if it be your will. Amen.

PRAYER OF DELIVERANE

Jesus, I come to you as my Deliverer. I believe that You are the Son of God, that You died for me and rose again. I confess You as Lord and renounce all influences of Satan in my life. Lord, you know the demons that oppress me, that harrass me, that entice me, that enslave me. I confess all my sins to You. (You must name them out loud before God).

I repent of (turn away from) all my sins. I renounce any form of the occult or idolatry in my life or in the life of my ancestors (Name them to the extent of your knowledge of it). I forgive anyone who has ever hurt me in any way and I let go of any bitterness or resentment. (Name any such people whom you associate with personal pain and forgive them by name).

I believe I am saved by the blood of Jesus, and Satan has no further legal rights to my spirit, soul, mind or body. Through the blood of Jesus I am justified, just as if I never sinned. Through the blood of Jesus I am sanctified, set apart to God. Through the blood of Jesus, I am redeemed out of the hand of the devil.

Jesus You said whoever calls upon the name of the Lord SHALL be delivered. I call upon You. Deliver me!

Now in the name of Jesus Christ I bind every evil spirit in or around my life. In the name of Jesus I command you to get out and leave me alone. Go in Jesus' name!

(Now cooperate with the Holy Spirit. It may help to breathe out. After expelling breath a few times, the enemy will begin to manifest and he will be forced to leave. Use your will to force him out in Jesus' name. Then praise God for the results and get filled with the Holy Spirit).

ABOUT THE AUTHOR

Robin Dinnanauth is an international evangelist and deliverance minister. He ministers the Gospel of the Lord Jesus Christ and demonstrates God's saving, healing and deliverance power throughout the United States and around the globe. He has been used mightily by God in the ministry of healing and deliverance. He is out on the front line, battling Satan and leading the charge against demonic forces that are destroying so many lives.

He is a highly sought-after crusader and revival speaker whom God has raised up as a prophetic voice to the world. Robin Dinnanauth is on a mission to bring the lost to the cross through the good news of the Gospel and the power of the blood of the Lamb. His Goal is to empower people through the Word of God, that they may discover the authority that God has given to them to subdue Satan's plan.

Thousands have experienced the saving, healing and delivering message of Jesus Christ as Robin Dinnanauth ministers hope to the sick, the afflicted and the hurting. He is known for his dynamic and anointed prayer, healing and deliverance ministry. He is an ordained minister, a CEO, pastor, overseer, mentor and founder of the Emmanuel Full

Gospel Assemblies of Churches, Robin Healing Ministries and RDM Institute of Spiritual Development.

He is also the author of Ambush the Enemy, Power to Prosper and so many other books and Spiritual Warfare Audio Recordings. For these and other media resources and tools by Robin Dinnanauth, you can visit RHM website at www.bishoprobin.com

SPIRITUAL WARFARE PRAYERS AND RESOURCESE FOR YOUR COMPLETE DELIVERANCE

Get my book *Call to Duty – Advance Warfare* and use the prayer in that book to conduct your deliverance. Also you can use the Call to Duty Advanced Warfare Prayer CD which can be a very great tool for your total deliverance. If you purchase the *Spiritual Warfare Healing and Deliverance Kit*, then it's all included there.

NOTES

.......END......

www.ingramcontent.com/pod-product-compliance
Ingram Content Group UK Ltd.
Pitfield, Milton Keynes, MK11 3LW, UK
UKHW041940190726
13854UKWH00004B/1694